THE SIMPLE PRAYER JOURNAL

A NOTEBOOK FOR MEN & TEEN BOYS

WRITTEN & DESIGNED BY SHALANA FRISBY

Don't forget to grab your bonus freebies today!

WWW.123JOURNALIT.COM / FREEBIES

SCRIPTURE FLASHCARDS – BIBLE READING PROMPTS – JOURNALING PAGES

More information at: www.123journalit.com

First Printing: May 2018
1 2 3 Journal It Publishing

ISBN-13: 978-1-947209-48-0
Pocketbook 6x9-in. Format Size
From the *Christian Workbooks* Series

THIS JOURNAL BELONGS TO

_ _ _ _ _ _ _ _

MY PRAYER NOTES FOR THE WEEK OF _____ TO _____

MONDAY:

TUESDAY:

WEDNESDAY:

THURSDAY:

FRIDAY:

SATURDAY:

SUNDAY:

ANSWERED PRAYERS & THINGS I'M THANKFUL FOR THIS WEEK:

MY PRAYER NOTES FOR THE WEEK OF _____ TO _____

MONDAY:

TUESDAY:

WEDNESDAY:

THURSDAY:

FRIDAY:

SATURDAY:

SUNDAY:

ANSWERED PRAYERS & THINGS I'M THANKFUL FOR THIS WEEK:

_____

_____

_____

_____

_____

_____

MY PRAYER NOTES FOR THE WEEK OF _____ TO _____

MONDAY:

TUESDAY:

WEDNESDAY:

THURSDAY:

FRIDAY:

SATURDAY:

SUNDAY:

ANSWERED PRAYERS & THINGS I'M THANKFUL FOR THIS WEEK:

MY PRAYER NOTES FOR THE WEEK OF _____ TO _____

MONDAY:

TUESDAY:

WEDNESDAY:

THURSDAY:

FRIDAY:

SATURDAY:

SUNDAY:

ANSWERED PRAYERS & THINGS I'M THANKFUL FOR THIS WEEK:

MY PRAYER NOTES FOR THE WEEK OF _____ TO _____

MONDAY:

TUESDAY:

WEDNESDAY:

THURSDAY:

FRIDAY:

SATURDAY:

SUNDAY:

ANSWERED PRAYERS & THINGS I'M THANKFUL FOR THIS WEEK:

MY PRAYER NOTES FOR THE WEEK OF _____ TO _____

MONDAY:

TUESDAY:

WEDNESDAY:

THURSDAY:

FRIDAY:

SATURDAY:

SUNDAY:

ANSWERED PRAYERS & THINGS I'M THANKFUL FOR THIS WEEK:

MY PRAYER NOTES FOR THE WEEK OF _____ TO _____

MONDAY:

TUESDAY:

WEDNESDAY:

THURSDAY:

FRIDAY:

SATURDAY:

SUNDAY:

ANSWERED PRAYERS & THINGS I'M THANKFUL FOR THIS WEEK:

_____
_____
_____
_____
_____
_____

MY PRAYER NOTES FOR THE WEEK OF _____ TO _____

MONDAY:

TUESDAY:

WEDNESDAY:

THURSDAY:

FRIDAY:

SATURDAY:

SUNDAY:

ANSWERED PRAYERS & THINGS I'M THANKFUL FOR THIS WEEK:

MY PRAYER NOTES FOR THE WEEK OF _____ TO _____

MONDAY:

TUESDAY:

WEDNESDAY:

THURSDAY:

FRIDAY:

SATURDAY:

SUNDAY:

ANSWERED PRAYERS & THINGS I'M THANKFUL FOR THIS WEEK:

MY PRAYER NOTES FOR THE WEEK OF _____ TO _____

MONDAY:

TUESDAY:

WEDNESDAY:

THURSDAY:

FRIDAY:

SATURDAY:

SUNDAY:

ANSWERED PRAYERS & THINGS I'M THANKFUL FOR THIS WEEK:

MY PRAYER NOTES FOR THE WEEK OF _____ TO _____

MONDAY:

TUESDAY:

WEDNESDAY:

THURSDAY:

FRIDAY:

SATURDAY:

SUNDAY:

ANSWERED PRAYERS & THINGS I'M THANKFUL FOR THIS WEEK:

MY PRAYER NOTES FOR THE WEEK OF _____ TO _____

MONDAY:

TUESDAY:

WEDNESDAY:

THURSDAY:

FRIDAY:

SATURDAY:

SUNDAY:

ANSWERED PRAYERS & THINGS I'M THANKFUL FOR THIS WEEK:

MY PRAYER NOTES FOR THE WEEK OF _____ TO _____

MONDAY:

TUESDAY:

WEDNESDAY:

THURSDAY:

FRIDAY:

SATURDAY:

SUNDAY:

ANSWERED PRAYERS & THINGS I'M THANKFUL FOR THIS WEEK:

MY PRAYER NOTES FOR THE WEEK OF _____ TO _____

MONDAY:

TUESDAY:

WEDNESDAY:

THURSDAY:

FRIDAY:

SATURDAY:

SUNDAY:

ANSWERED PRAYERS & THINGS I'M THANKFUL FOR THIS WEEK:

MY PRAYER NOTES FOR THE WEEK OF _____ TO _____

MONDAY:

TUESDAY:

WEDNESDAY:

THURSDAY:

FRIDAY:

SATURDAY:

SUNDAY:

ANSWERED PRAYERS & THINGS I'M THANKFUL FOR THIS WEEK:

MY PRAYER NOTES FOR THE WEEK OF _____ TO _____

MONDAY:

TUESDAY:

WEDNESDAY:

THURSDAY:

FRIDAY:

SATURDAY:

SUNDAY:

ANSWERED PRAYERS & THINGS I'M THANKFUL FOR THIS WEEK:

MY PRAYER NOTES FOR THE WEEK OF _____ TO _____

MONDAY:

TUESDAY:

WEDNESDAY:

THURSDAY:

FRIDAY:

SATURDAY:

SUNDAY:

ANSWERED PRAYERS & THINGS I'M THANKFUL FOR THIS WEEK:

MY PRAYER NOTES FOR THE WEEK OF _____ TO _____

MONDAY:

TUESDAY:

WEDNESDAY:

THURSDAY:

FRIDAY:

SATURDAY:

SUNDAY:

ANSWERED PRAYERS & THINGS I'M THANKFUL FOR THIS WEEK:

MY PRAYER NOTES FOR THE WEEK OF _____ TO _____

MONDAY:

TUESDAY:

WEDNESDAY:

THURSDAY:

FRIDAY:

SATURDAY:

SUNDAY:

ANSWERED PRAYERS & THINGS I'M THANKFUL FOR THIS WEEK:

MY PRAYER NOTES FOR THE WEEK OF _____ TO _____

MONDAY:

TUESDAY:

WEDNESDAY:

THURSDAY:

FRIDAY:

SATURDAY:

SUNDAY:

ANSWERED PRAYERS & THINGS I'M THANKFUL FOR THIS WEEK:

MY PRAYER NOTES FOR THE WEEK OF _____ TO _____

MONDAY:

TUESDAY:

WEDNESDAY:

THURSDAY:

FRIDAY:

SATURDAY:

SUNDAY:

ANSWERED PRAYERS & THINGS I'M THANKFUL FOR THIS WEEK:

MY PRAYER NOTES FOR THE WEEK OF _____ TO _____

MONDAY:

TUESDAY:

WEDNESDAY:

THURSDAY:

FRIDAY:

SATURDAY:

SUNDAY:

ANSWERED PRAYERS & THINGS I'M THANKFUL FOR THIS WEEK:

MY PRAYER NOTES FOR THE WEEK OF _____ TO _____

MONDAY:

TUESDAY:

WEDNESDAY:

THURSDAY:

FRIDAY:

SATURDAY:

SUNDAY:

ANSWERED PRAYERS & THINGS I'M THANKFUL FOR THIS WEEK:

_____
_____
_____
_____
_____
_____

MY PRAYER NOTES FOR THE WEEK OF _____ TO _____

MONDAY:

TUESDAY:

WEDNESDAY:

THURSDAY:

FRIDAY:

SATURDAY:

SUNDAY:

ANSWERED PRAYERS & THINGS I'M THANKFUL FOR THIS WEEK:

MY PRAYER NOTES FOR THE WEEK OF _____ TO _____

MONDAY:

TUESDAY:

WEDNESDAY:

THURSDAY:

FRIDAY:

SATURDAY:

SUNDAY:

ANSWERED PRAYERS & THINGS I'M THANKFUL FOR THIS WEEK:

MY PRAYER NOTES FOR THE WEEK OF _____ TO _____

MONDAY:

TUESDAY:

WEDNESDAY:

THURSDAY:

FRIDAY:

SATURDAY:

SUNDAY:

ANSWERED PRAYERS & THINGS I'M THANKFUL FOR THIS WEEK:

MY PRAYER NOTES FOR THE WEEK OF _____ TO _____

MONDAY:

TUESDAY:

WEDNESDAY:

THURSDAY:

FRIDAY:

SATURDAY:

SUNDAY:

ANSWERED PRAYERS & THINGS I'M THANKFUL FOR THIS WEEK:

MY PRAYER NOTES FOR THE WEEK OF _____ TO _____

MONDAY:

TUESDAY:

WEDNESDAY:

THURSDAY:

FRIDAY:

SATURDAY:

SUNDAY:

ANSWERED PRAYERS & THINGS I'M THANKFUL FOR THIS WEEK:

MY PRAYER NOTES FOR THE WEEK OF _____ TO _____

MONDAY:

TUESDAY:

WEDNESDAY:

THURSDAY:

FRIDAY:

SATURDAY:

SUNDAY:

ANSWERED PRAYERS & THINGS I'M THANKFUL FOR THIS WEEK:

MY PRAYER NOTES FOR THE WEEK OF _____ TO _____

MONDAY:

TUESDAY:

WEDNESDAY:

THURSDAY:

FRIDAY:

SATURDAY:

SUNDAY:

ANSWERED PRAYERS & THINGS I'M THANKFUL FOR THIS WEEK:

MY PRAYER NOTES FOR THE WEEK OF _____ TO _____

MONDAY:

TUESDAY:

WEDNESDAY:

THURSDAY:

FRIDAY:

SATURDAY:

SUNDAY:

ANSWERED PRAYERS & THINGS I'M THANKFUL FOR THIS WEEK:

MY PRAYER NOTES FOR THE WEEK OF _____ TO _____

MONDAY:

TUESDAY:

WEDNESDAY:

THURSDAY:

FRIDAY:

- -
- -
- -
- -

SATURDAY:

- -
- -
- -
- -

SUNDAY:

- -
- -
- -
- -

ANSWERED PRAYERS & THINGS I'M THANKFUL FOR THIS WEEK:

MY PRAYER NOTES FOR THE WEEK OF _____ TO _____

MONDAY:

TUESDAY:

WEDNESDAY:

THURSDAY:

FRIDAY:

SATURDAY:

SUNDAY:

ANSWERED PRAYERS & THINGS I'M THANKFUL FOR THIS WEEK:

MY PRAYER NOTES FOR THE WEEK OF _____ TO _____

MONDAY:

TUESDAY:

WEDNESDAY:

THURSDAY:

FRIDAY:

SATURDAY:

SUNDAY:

ANSWERED PRAYERS & THINGS I'M THANKFUL FOR THIS WEEK:

MY PRAYER NOTES FOR THE WEEK OF _____ TO _____

MONDAY:

TUESDAY:

WEDNESDAY:

THURSDAY:

FRIDAY:

SATURDAY:

SUNDAY:

ANSWERED PRAYERS & THINGS I'M THANKFUL FOR THIS WEEK:

MY PRAYER NOTES FOR THE WEEK OF _____ TO _____

MONDAY:

TUESDAY:

WEDNESDAY:

THURSDAY:

FRIDAY:

SATURDAY:

SUNDAY:

ANSWERED PRAYERS & THINGS I'M THANKFUL FOR THIS WEEK:

MY PRAYER NOTES FOR THE WEEK OF _____ TO _____

MONDAY:

TUESDAY:

WEDNESDAY:

THURSDAY:

FRIDAY:

SATURDAY:

SUNDAY:

ANSWERED PRAYERS & THINGS I'M THANKFUL FOR THIS WEEK:

_____

_____

_____

_____

_____

_____

MY PRAYER NOTES FOR THE WEEK OF _____ TO _____

MONDAY:

TUESDAY:

WEDNESDAY:

THURSDAY:

FRIDAY:

SATURDAY:

SUNDAY:

ANSWERED PRAYERS & THINGS I'M THANKFUL FOR THIS WEEK:

MY PRAYER NOTES FOR THE WEEK OF _____ TO _____

MONDAY:

TUESDAY:

WEDNESDAY:

THURSDAY:

FRIDAY:

_____

_____

_____

_____

SATURDAY:

_____

_____

_____

_____

SUNDAY:

_____

_____

_____

_____

ANSWERED PRAYERS & THINGS I'M THANKFUL FOR THIS WEEK:

_____

_____

_____

_____

_____

_____

MY PRAYER NOTES FOR THE WEEK OF _____ TO _____

MONDAY:

TUESDAY:

WEDNESDAY:

THURSDAY:

FRIDAY:

SATURDAY:

SUNDAY:

ANSWERED PRAYERS & THINGS I'M THANKFUL FOR THIS WEEK:

MY PRAYER NOTES FOR THE WEEK OF _____ TO _____

MONDAY:

TUESDAY:

WEDNESDAY:

THURSDAY:

FRIDAY:

SATURDAY:

SUNDAY:

ANSWERED PRAYERS & THINGS I'M THANKFUL FOR THIS WEEK:

MY PRAYER NOTES FOR THE WEEK OF _____ TO _____

MONDAY:

TUESDAY:

WEDNESDAY:

THURSDAY:

FRIDAY:

SATURDAY:

SUNDAY:

ANSWERED PRAYERS & THINGS I'M THANKFUL FOR THIS WEEK:

MY PRAYER NOTES FOR THE WEEK OF _____ TO _____

MONDAY:

TUESDAY:

WEDNESDAY:

THURSDAY:

FRIDAY:

SATURDAY:

SUNDAY:

ANSWERED PRAYERS & THINGS I'M THANKFUL FOR THIS WEEK:

MY PRAYER NOTES FOR THE WEEK OF _____ TO _____

MONDAY:

TUESDAY:

WEDNESDAY:

THURSDAY:

FRIDAY:

- -
- -
- -
- -

SATURDAY:

- -
- -
- -
- -

SUNDAY:

- -
- -
- -

ANSWERED PRAYERS & THINGS I'M THANKFUL FOR THIS WEEK:

MY PRAYER NOTES FOR THE WEEK OF _____ TO _____

MONDAY:

TUESDAY:

WEDNESDAY:

THURSDAY:

FRIDAY:

SATURDAY:

SUNDAY:

ANSWERED PRAYERS & THINGS I'M THANKFUL FOR THIS WEEK:

MY PRAYER NOTES FOR THE WEEK OF _____ TO _____

MONDAY:

TUESDAY:

WEDNESDAY:

THURSDAY:

FRIDAY:

SATURDAY:

SUNDAY:

ANSWERED PRAYERS & THINGS I'M THANKFUL FOR THIS WEEK:

MY PRAYER NOTES FOR THE WEEK OF _____ TO _____

MONDAY:

TUESDAY:

WEDNESDAY:

THURSDAY:

FRIDAY:

SATURDAY:

SUNDAY:

ANSWERED PRAYERS & THINGS I'M THANKFUL FOR THIS WEEK:

MY PRAYER NOTES FOR THE WEEK OF _____ TO _____

MONDAY:

TUESDAY:

WEDNESDAY:

THURSDAY:

FRIDAY:

SATURDAY:

SUNDAY:

ANSWERED PRAYERS & THINGS I'M THANKFUL FOR THIS WEEK:

MY PRAYER NOTES FOR THE WEEK OF _____ TO _____

MONDAY:

TUESDAY:

WEDNESDAY:

THURSDAY:

FRIDAY:

SATURDAY:

SUNDAY:

ANSWERED PRAYERS & THINGS I'M THANKFUL FOR THIS WEEK:

MY PRAYER NOTES FOR THE WEEK OF _____ TO _____

MONDAY:

TUESDAY:

WEDNESDAY:

THURSDAY:

FRIDAY:

SATURDAY:

SUNDAY:

ANSWERED PRAYERS & THINGS I'M THANKFUL FOR THIS WEEK:

MY PRAYER NOTES FOR THE WEEK OF _____ TO _____

MONDAY:

TUESDAY:

WEDNESDAY:

THURSDAY:

FRIDAY:

SATURDAY:

SUNDAY:

ANSWERED PRAYERS & THINGS I'M THANKFUL FOR THIS WEEK:

MY PRAYER NOTES FOR THE WEEK OF _____ TO _____

MONDAY:
- -
- -
- -
- -

TUESDAY:
- -
- -
- -
- -

WEDNESDAY:
- -
- -
- -
- -

THURSDAY:
- -
- -
- -
- -

FRIDAY:

SATURDAY:

SUNDAY:

ANSWERED PRAYERS & THINGS I'M THANKFUL FOR THIS WEEK:

Printed in Great Britain
by Amazon

11623358R00068